A first guide to

Germany

By Kath Davies

A ZOË BOOK

Devised and produced by
Zoë Books Limited
15 Worthy Lane
Winchester
Hampshire SO23 7AB
England

Illustrative material used in this book first appeared in *Discovering Germany*, published by Zoë Books Limited.

First published in Great Britain in 1994 by
Zoë Books Limited
15 Worthy Lane
Winchester
Hampshire SO23 7AB

A record of the CIP data is available from the British Library.

ISBN 1 874488 33 9

Printed in Italy by Grafedit SpA
Design: Jan Sterling, Sterling Associates
Picture research: Suzanne Williams
Editor: Donna Bailey
Map: Gecko Limited
Production: Grahame Griffiths

Photographic acknowledgments

The publishers wish to acknowledge, with thanks, the following photographic sources:

Cover: Lesley & Roy Adkins Picture Library; title page: Tony Stone Images; 5 Robert Harding Picture Library; 6,7l Zefa; 7r Robert Harding Picture Library; 8 Zefa; 9l Robert Harding Picture Library; 9r,10 Zefa; 11l Staatsarchiv, Hamburg/Bridgeman Art Library; 11r Zefa; 12 Frank Spooner Pictures; 13l Robert Harding Picture Library; 13r a detail from the cathedral scene from *Faust* 'Margaret tormented by the evil spirits' by Frank Cadogan Cowper, Private Collection/Bridgeman Art Library; 14 Zefa; 15,16 Robert Harding Picture Library; 17l Zefa; 17r,18 Robert Harding Picture Library; 19l,19r Zefa; 20,21,22 Robert Harding Picture Library; 23,24 Zefa; 25 Musée Condé Chantilly, Giraudon/Bridgeman Art Library; 26 Neill Bruce Photographic; 27l,27r Rex Features; 28 Frank Spooner Pictures; 29l Rex Features; 29r Frank Spooner Pictures.

Cover: *The town square in Bernkastel, in the Rhineland–Palatinate*

Title page: *Cochem, on the River Moselle*

Contents

German words are shown in *italics* and are explained in the text.

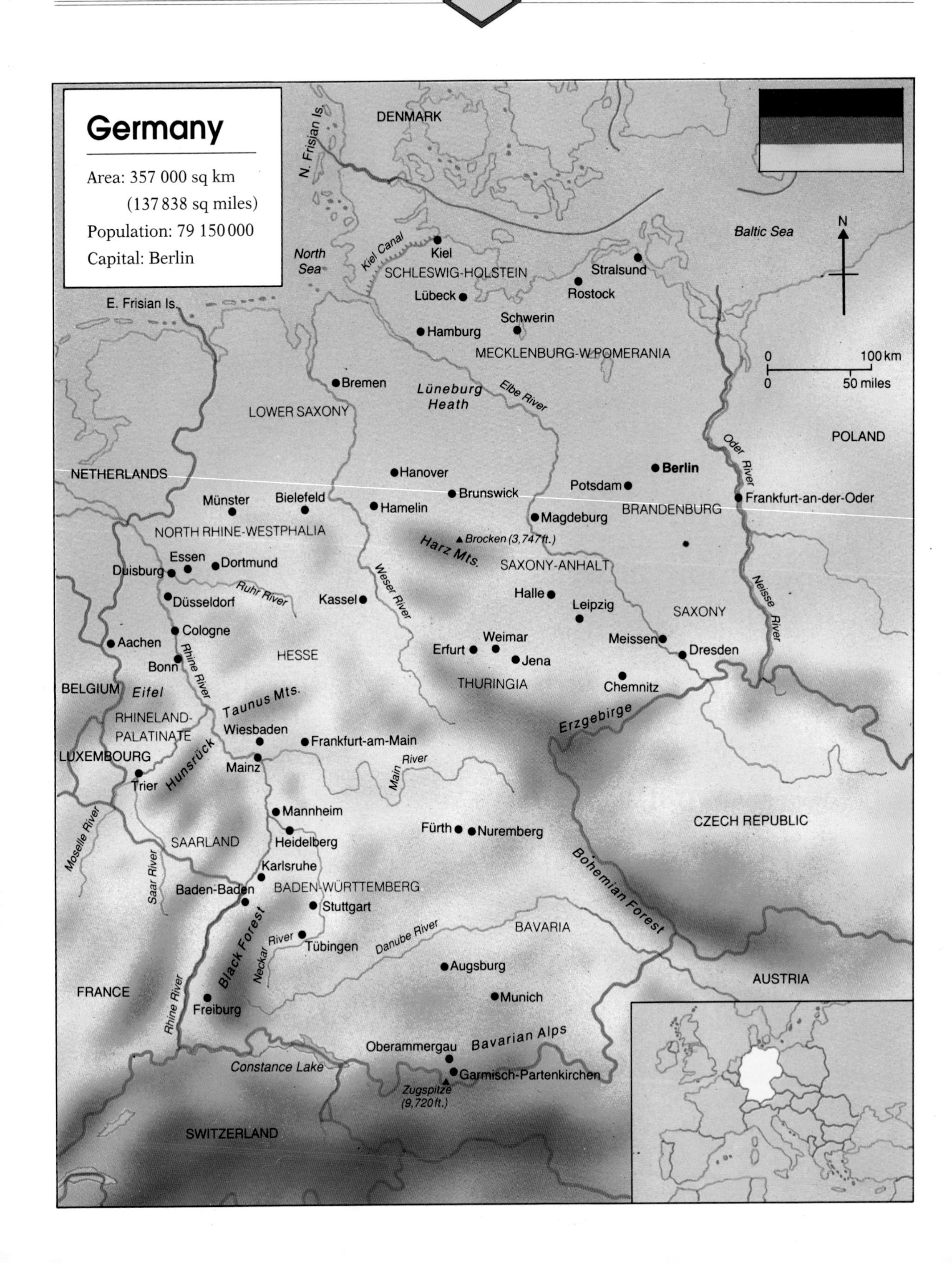
Germany
Area: 357 000 sq km
(137 838 sq miles)
Population: 79 150 000
Capital: Berlin
DENMARK
N. Frisian Is.
North Sea
Kiel Canal
Kiel
SCHLESWIG-HOLSTEIN
Baltic Sea
Stralsund
Rostock
Lübeck
E. Frisian Is.
Schwerin
Hamburg
MECKLENBURG-W.POMERANIA
0
100 km
0
50 miles
Bremen
Lüneburg Heath
Elbe River
LOWER SAXONY
Oder River
POLAND
NETHERLANDS
Hanover
Berlin
Potsdam
Brunswick
Münster
Bielefeld
Hamelin
Frankfurt-an-der-Oder
Magdeburg
BRANDENBURG
NORTH RHINE-WESTPHALIA
Brocken (3,747 ft.)
Harz Mts.
Essen
Dortmund
SAXONY-ANHALT
Duisburg
Weser River
Neisse River
Ruhr River
Halle
Düsseldorf
Kassel
Leipzig
SAXONY
Cologne
Weimar
Meissen
Aachen
Erfurt
Jena
Dresden
HESSE
Rhine River
Bonn
THURINGIA
Chemnitz
BELGIUM
Eifel
Taunus Mts.
Erzgebirge
RHINELAND-PALATINATE
Wiesbaden
Frankfurt-am-Main
LUXEMBOURG
Hunsrück
Mainz
Main River
Trier
Mannheim
CZECH REPUBLIC
Moselle River
Fürth
Nuremberg
SAARLAND
Heidelberg
Saar River
Karlsruhe
Bohemian Forest
Baden-Baden
BADEN-WÜRTTEMBERG
Stuttgart
BAVARIA
Black Forest
Neckar River
Tübingen
Danube River
Augsburg
AUSTRIA
FRANCE
Rhine River
Munich
Freiburg
Bavarian Alps
Oberammergau
Constance Lake
Garmisch-Partenkirchen
Zugspitze (9,720 ft.)
SWITZERLAND

Welcome!

Wilkommen – Welcome to Germany!

Germany is a large country in the centre of northern Europe. It stretches from the cold, grey waves of the North Sea and the Baltic Sea, to the Bavarian Alps on the Swiss and Austrian borders.

Germany is divided into 16 states called *Länder*. The *Länder* make their own laws, but they also join together under one central government.

There are many different regions of Germany.

Everybody speaks German, but people in different *Länder* may speak a local dialect or form of German. Children at school learn High German, or *Hochdeutsch*. High German is used in business and newspapers, on radio and television.

Two countries

Between 1945 and 1990 the ten *Länder* of the Federal Republic of Germany (FRG) in the west were divided from the eastern states of the German Democratic Republic (GDR). A barbed wire frontier guarded by soldiers and a wall through Berlin separated the two countries. Today Germany is no longer divided. It is one nation again.

◀ In 1989 many people joined in to help knock down the wall that divided Berlin.

Along the Rhine

The River Rhine flows north from the Swiss border to the North Sea. It is 1326 kilometres (823 miles) long. This broad, winding river passes between steep banks until it enters the plains of north Germany at Cologne. Many small villages and castles border the river.

There are many stories about the Rhine. One legend tells how the songs of a beautiful woman called the Lorelei lured sailors to their death on the rocks in the river.

The River Rhine has been used by traders for thousands of years. Today it is still busy with barges. It takes eight days to carry goods from Basel in Switzerland along the river to the mouth of the Rhine at Rotterdam in the Netherlands.

▼ The River Rhine at Pfalz, where there was once a customs post.

▲ Checking the quality of the wine stored in the barrels

Wine and beer

The Romans were the first people to plant grape vines along the valley of the Rhine. Today, vines still grow on the slopes of the upper Rhine valley. When the grapes are harvested in September, many farming villages hold festivals. Further north in the country, people brew beer.

The lower Rhine

From the quiet university town of Bonn, the Rhine flows north to Cologne and Düsseldorf, a centre of the arts, business and entertainment. A carnival is held in Düsseldorf in spring every year.

The world's largest inland port is at Duisburg. There are many coal mines, steel works and factories in this area, called the Ruhr. In the past their waste dirtied the waters of the Rhine. Today the factories are cleaner, but pollution is still a problem.

▼ Cologne Cathedral

Forests and mountains

The Black Forest in Germany's south-west corner is a region of wooded hills, meadows and old farmhouses. The River Neckar crosses this region. On its banks are the old university towns of Heidelberg and Tübingen, and the industrial town of Stuttgart.

In the south, on the Swiss border, lies Lake Constance, or *Bodensee*. To the east is Bavaria and its beautiful old towns. One of these is Nuremburg which is famous for toy-making and for gingerbread. The capital of Bavaria is Munich, a centre for industry and the arts.

▼ Farmhouses in the Black Forest

▲ Skiing in southern Germany

Snow and sun

Zugspitze, the highest peak in the Bavarian Alps, rises to 2962 metres (9718 feet). Deep snow covers the mountains in winter. Many people come to the Alps to ski and to take part in winter sports.

In summer the farmers lead their cattle to the high alpine meadows to graze on the rich grass. In autumn the cattle return to the farms. They spend all the winter in barns.

Alpine farmhouses are made of wood with sloping roofs. Many of them are carved or painted.

▲ Neuschwanstein Castle

Fairy-tale castles

King Ludwig II ruled Bavaria from 1864 until 1886. He loved music and tales of long ago. He built several castles in Bavaria. The most famous of these is Neuschwanstein Castle.

The centre and the north

▲ The River Main flows through Frankfurt.

Frankfurt is the largest city in the *Land* of Hesse. It was the birthplace of the famous poet, Johann Wolfgang von Goethe. Frankfurt has many banks, businesses and offices. Its airport is one of the busiest in Europe. People from all over the world visit its trade fairs. They come to see the furniture, books or cars on show there.

Kassel, the capital of Hesse, has a museum about Jakob and Wilhelm Grimm. Their fairy stories, such as 'Little Red Riding Hood', are known all over the world.

Another folk tale 'The Pied Piper' is based on the town of Hamelin in Lower Saxony. It tells how a piper charmed away the city's rats. When the mayor would not pay him, the piper took away the children too.

Trading cities

More than 400 years ago, the cities of northern Europe set up an organisation called the Hanseatic League. Their merchants owned warehouses for goods in cities from London to Moscow. Cities in the League became rich and powerful. Many of them, such as Hamburg and Bremen, are still important trading centres.

▼ Merchants of Hamburg in the days of the Hanseatic League

▲ A beach on the north coast

The northern coasts

People come to spend their holidays on Germany's northern coasts and beaches. They sail, swim and watch birds. Offshore, the Friesian Islands welcome many visitors. The Friesian people have their own language and customs.

The *Land* in the north of Germany is called Schleswig-Holstein. It is a narrow strip of land between the North Sea and the Baltic Sea. The Kiel Canal linking the two seas is 100 kilometres (62 miles) long. It is the busiest canal in the world. There are large ports at Kiel and at Lübeck.

Eastern Germany

The River Elbe is the most important river of eastern Germany. It flows north-west for 1165 kilometres (723 miles) from its source in the Czech Republic to its mouth at Hamburg on the North Sea. In the south, the Elbe flows through Dresden and Meissen, the centre for fine German china. This region of south-east Germany has many coal mines and steel works centred around cities such as Leipzig, Magdeburg and Halle. Smoke and dirt from these industries still pollutes the air in this region.

▼ A power station in the region south of Leipzig

Dresden is the capital of the *Land* of Saxony. Dresden is one of Germany's most beautiful cities. It was destroyed by the worst bombing raid of the Second World War. Many of the city's buildings have been carefully rebuilt.

Germany's north-east corner is a region of vast plains. Here the River Oder and the River Neisse mark the border with Poland. South-west of Magdeburg is the hilly country of the Harz Mountains, where many valuable metals are mined.

▼ Dresden castle was built between 1630 and 1701.

▲ This scene from Goethe's *Faust* shows an evil spirit tormenting a woman.

Some of the villages of the Harz mountains are hundreds of years old. It is said that witches come to the area to dance on Mayday Eve.

Another famous story from the region is about Doctor Faust. He is said to have sold his soul to the devil in return for knowledge and power. Germany's famous writer Johann Wolfgang von Goethe wrote a play about Faust.

Berlin

▲ The Brandenburg gate is at the centre of Berlin.

More than three million people live in Berlin. It is the capital city of Germany. Berlin lies on the plains of north-east Germany. It covers an area of 880 square kilometres (339 square miles).

During the Second World War, many fine buildings were destroyed, but they have since been rebuilt. Between 1945 and 1990 the city was divided in half. The western half was in the Federal Republic of Germany. The eastern half was in the German Democratic Republic. In 1961 the GDR built a wall across the city. People who tried to cross the wall were shot. In 1989 the wall was taken down. Berliners celebrated as their city became one again.

Sights to see

The Tiergarten is Berlin's largest park. It stretches from the Brandenburg gate to Berlin's famous zoo.

The Memorial Church is a famous landmark. The Church was bombed during the Second World War. Now only a ruined tower is left.

Charlottenburg is a royal palace which is 300 years old. There are paintings and tapestries inside, and a fine garden outside the palace.

Shops and streets

Berlin's districts are linked by an underground railway, the *U- bahn*. The city centre has wide streets. The *Kurfürstendamm* (known to all as the *Ku'damm*) is famous for its shops. *Unter den Linden*, one of the most famous avenues in the world, stretches from the royal palace to the Brandenburg Gate. This massive arch in the centre of Berlin was built in 1784.

Young people like to go to the Kreuzberg district. Here they listen to the new bands and dance at the night clubs. They meet in the cafés to talk about art, politics and the latest fashions.

Many Berliners live in the outer suburbs in high-rise flats. On summer weekends they like to escape to the many lakes, rivers and woods which surround the city.

▼ The bright lights of *Ku'damm*

People at work

Germany is one of the most important industrial countries in Europe. In the past, mining, iron and steel works were important industries. Today people also make cars and trucks, and work in the chemical, textile and electronic industries. Companies such as Volkswagen, BMW and Bosch are famous all over the world.

German people are well trained and work hard. More Germans now work in shops, banks and offices than in mines or factories. Nearly half of Germany's workers are women. They play an important part in industry, business and politics. Many German workers belong to trades unions. They help to decide how their firms are run.

▼ A German car factory

▲ Haymaking in the Bavarian Alps

In the countryside

Only a few Germans still work on the land. Many of their farms are very small. All members of the family help on the farm. They may also have jobs in the nearest town.

The farmers have machines to help them do most of their work. They grow large crops of wheat, barley, potatoes and sugar beet. They also keep beef and dairy cattle, sheep and chickens. Their pigs provide meat for sausages and other special German dishes.

Shops and markets

Germans do most of their shopping at large out-of-town supermarkets. In the city centres, there are big department stores and small corner shops. Street markets sell fresh flowers, fruit, vegetables, and many other goods. Many cities have special Christmas markets, which have been held in the same places for hundreds of years.

▼ A street market at Tübingen

Everyday life

German children start their school day at eight o'clock. Lessons are over at 1 pm, and most children go home for lunch. Older children may return to school in the afternoon for study and activity groups. In the summer pupils may go swimming. In the winter they go skating. After lessons, and in the school holidays, many children meet friends at youth clubs. The clubs have indoor games and sports, discos and rock concerts.

▼ Learning English at school

Town and around

Fast motorways, or *autobahnen*, link the main towns and cities throughout Germany.

Most Germans live in the suburbs of towns and cities. Trains and buses link the suburbs with the city centres. The people live in flats on housing estates, or in houses with small gardens.

Many cities have parks and green areas around them where people can relax and play sports. At weekends the parks are full of people cycling or jogging.

▼ A family jogging in the park

▲ Swimming in the local pool

Keeping fit

Children do not play sport at school. Many German children join local sports clubs to keep fit. Swimming, athletics, horse-riding and tennis are very popular. The most popular sport is football. Teams such as Bayern Munich are among the best in Europe.

Enjoy your meal!

▲ Fresh bread and cakes in a German bakery

German bakers make many different kinds of bread. There are crusty rolls and loaves flavoured with poppy seeds or caraway. Breads made from rye include dark, heavy loaves called *Pumpernickel*. This bread tastes good with cheese or thin slices of ham.

Germany is famous for its cakes and pies, such as cherry tart. On Sundays people often visit their relatives for coffee. They buy cakes to take with them.

Traditional food

German food is filling and tasty. Soups are made from onions, peas and beans. Favourite meats include pork served with potatoes or dumplings, and perhaps with spinach or a pickled cabbage called *Sauerkraut*. In the north, people enjoy fish, especially herring and eels.

Super sausages

It is said that more than 1500 sausages or *wurst* are made in Germany! Some are boiled, such as *Weisswurst*. Others are grilled, like *Bratwurst*. German butchers also sell cold meats, such as salamis and smoked hams. Cold meats and breads are often served for a light supper in the evening.

▼ A display of German sausages outside a butcher's shop

Festivals and the arts

Festivals and fairs are held all over Germany throughout the year. In the Rhineland, children parade through the streets with lanterns on St Martin's Day, 11 November. In the south there is a carnival in spring called *Fasching*. In some regions there are parades with drums, rattles, ribbons and carved wooden masks.

Munich is famous for its beer festival, the *Oktoberfest*, held in autumn. People wear the costumes of their local region in the parade.

On 5 December, all over Germany, Saint Nicholas brings small presents for the children. The main celebration is on 24 December, Christmas Eve, when families gather around the Christmas tree. The idea of a decorated tree comes from Germany.

▼ Children dancing at a festival in Dinkelsbühl

▲ A scene at the opera in Munich

Land of music

Many of the greatest musicians are German. They include Johann Sebastian Bach, Ludwig van Beethoven and Johannes Brahms. Their music is played by famous orchestras such as the Berlin Philharmonic.

The music festival held in the Bavarian town of Bayreuth every year presents operas by Richard Wagner. Many of his operas retell old German myths and folk tales.

Folk dancing and brass bands are popular. Most young people listen to rock music. Many play in their own bands.

Art galleries

Museums and art galleries in Germany show the works of great artists such as Albrecht Dürer and Hans Holbein. They also show more modern works and the bold, colourful pictures of Expressionist artists. Smaller galleries show new work by modern artists and sculptors.

Writers and publishers

Books have always been important in Germany. About 1450, Johann Gutenberg of Mainz invented the first printing press in Europe with movable metal type. Today books by authors such as Thomas Mann and the plays of Bertolt Brecht are enjoyed worldwide.

Leipzig is the traditional centre of German book trade. In autumn, the world's largest book fair is held in Frankfurt.

Germany in history

Thousands of years ago, Germany was covered by thick forests. People called Celts lived here. In 1968, a Celtic chief's grave was found in the Black Forest. He was dressed in gold.

About 2500 years ago, people from the north and east drove out the Celts. These new people spoke a language called Germanic. They were the ancestors of the people who live in Germany today.

The Romans invaded the south and west of Germany about 2000 years ago. They built many towns and forts and they planted vines. Roman remains can be seen in towns such as Cologne and Mainz.

The Romans tried to take control of north and east Germany, but they were defeated by the German leader Hermann (Arminius) in AD 9. German armies, led by Odovacar, invaded Italy and conquered Rome in AD 476.

▼ A rebuilt Stone Age village from about 5000 BC on Lake Constance

▲ A bronze statue of Charlemagne

Charlemagne

The Franks set up a Germanic kingdom in France. Their Christian ruler Charlemagne enlarged the Frankish empire. He conquered the Saxons and Friesians in north Germany, the Bavarians in the south, and he invaded Italy. Charlemagne was crowned Emperor of Rome in AD 800.

The Holy Roman Empire

After Charlemagne died, the western part of his empire became France, and the eastern part Germany. Otto I, a Saxon king, set up the Holy Roman Empire. It lasted for 800 years. The Emperors were chosen by the German princes or Electors.

A changing world

About 500 years ago Germany was a land of castles and monasteries. Poets and scholars travelled around the country. Most people worked on the land. Craft workers, bankers and merchants became very rich.

Catholic and Protestant

Many people in Germany protested about the way the Roman Catholic Church was run. These Protestants were led by Martin Luther. Some Electors agreed with Luther. Others followed the Emperor, a Catholic. The war between them lasted for thirty years.

United – and divided

After the Thirty Years' War, Germany was broken into many small states. Under King Frederick the Great (1712-1786), the Protestant state of Prussia became one of the most powerful states in Europe. France invaded Prussia in 1806, but in 1815 Prussia joined with Britain against France. They defeated the French at the battle of Waterloo.

The German states united to make a single country in 1871. King Wilhelm I of Prussia was crowned the first emperor or *Kaiser* of Germany.

During the 1800s German engineers and inventors had great success. Gottlieb Daimler built the first petrol-driven motor cycle. Benz designed the first petrol-engined motor car.

▼ Gottlieb Daimler's petrol-engined motor cycle

▲ In the 1930s many young Germans joined Nazi groups.

The First World War

The German empire spread. It seized countries in Africa. The *Kaiser* wanted to rule Europe. In 1914 his armies attacked Belgium and France and the First World War began. Millions of people were killed. Germany was defeated in 1918 and the *Kaiser* fled to Holland.

After the war many people were out of work. They did not have enough money to buy food or fuel.

The Nazi Party

In 1933 Adolf Hitler, leader of the Nazi Party, became the Chancellor of Germany. The Nazis put people in prison or killed those who did not agree with them. In 1939 Hitler led Germany into the Second World War. Germany was defeated in 1945. People found out that the Nazis had murdered more than 6 million Jewish people in terrible death camps.

Germany divided

After the war Germany was divided into two countries, the FRG and the GDR. Germany was united again in 1990.

▼ The Berlin Wall before 1989

Germany today

▲ East Germans at a political meeting

The new united Germany had many problems. Many people in the east lost their jobs. They felt they were not treated as well as Germans living in the west. Many people in the west were afraid that the east Germans would take their jobs.

Different political parties argue about how to solve Germany's problems. Some use violence to try to bring change. A few people have tried to bring back the ideas of the Nazi party. Most Germans are against these ideas.

A better future

Many people have come from other countries to live and work in Germany. Most Germans have welcomed these people but a few have attacked them. The German government is trying to stop these attacks.

Germany is an important member of the European Union, a group of 12 European nations. The countries of the EU work together to make trade between the members easier. They also want all people in the EU to have the same opportunities.

▼ Many east Germans could not afford to buy these toys for their children.

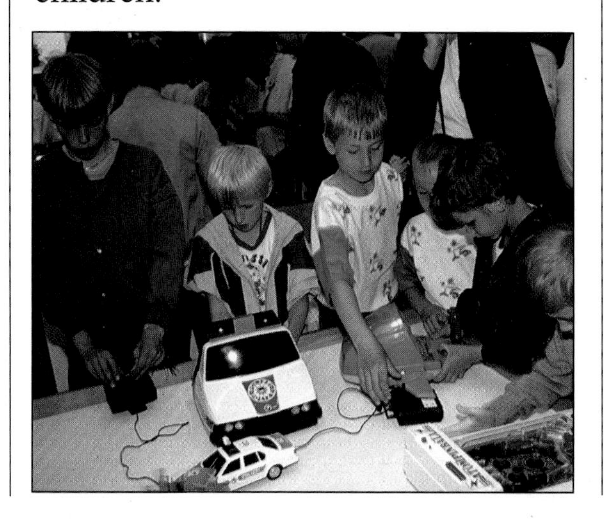

▲ Protesting against nuclear power

Most German people care for the environment. The Green Party is an important political party in Germany. Its members believe that people should think much more about pollution and recycling. Some Germans also dislike nuclear power. Young Germans, like other people, want to grow up in a peaceful, healthy and fairer world.

Fact file

Government

Germany is a democracy. The Germans elect or choose their rulers. The President, the head of state, is elected every five years. The German Parliament is called the *Bundestag*. It is elected every four years. The leader of the government is called the Chancellor. Each *Land* has its own regional government. The *Länder* send people called delegates to the central or federal council, the *Bundesrat*.

Flag

The German flag is black, red and gold. The colours were first worn by German soldiers who fought against the French in the 1800s.

Anthem

The national anthem is called 'Unity, Right and Freedom'. The music was written by Joseph Haydn in 1797.

Money

German money is called the *Deutsche Mark* (DM). It is divided into 100 *Pfennig* (pf).

Education

Children start school at the age of 6. At 11 they go to secondary school. In some *Länder* all children go to comprehensive schools called *Gesamtschulen*. In other *Länder* children may go to schools where they learn a trade. There are also technical colleges. Pupils go to these at the age of 15 or 16. Children who go to grammar schools, called *Gymnasien*, stay until they are 20. They take a final exam, the *Abitur*, before they go on to university.

Religion

Most Germans are Christians. Catholics live mostly in the south and west. Protestants live in the north and east.

Some famous people

Hildegard of Bingen (1098-1179) was an abbess, poet, musician and playwright.
Johann Gutenberg (1400-1468) pioneered printing.
Albrecht Dürer (1471-1528) was an artist and print-maker.
Martin Luther (1483-1546) was a Protestant who wanted to reform the Catholic Church.
Johann Kepler (1571-1630) studied the stars and planets.
Johann Sebastian Bach (1685-1750) was a composer.
Caroline Herschel (1750-1848) studied the stars and discovered 18 comets.
Ludwig van Beethoven (1770-1827) was a composer.
Georg Simon Ohm (1787-1854) studied electricity.
Clara Schumann (1819-1896) was a pianist.
Käthe Kollwitz (1867-1945) was a sculptor and painter.
Albert Einstein (1879-1955) was a mathematician and philosopher.

Some key events in history

AD **9**: Hermann (Arminius) defeated the Romans.
800: Charlemagne was crowned Emperor of Rome.
936: Otto I was crowned King of the Germans.
1241: North German merchants joined together and later formed the Hanseatic League.
1517: Martin Luther declared his Protestant beliefs.
1618-1648: Thirty Years' War
1712: Birth of Frederick the Great, King of Prussia
1806: Prussia defeated France.
1871: William I of Prussia became emperor of united Germany.
1914-1918: First World War
1933: Hitler became Chancellor.
1939-1945: Second World War
1949: Germany was divided into the GDR and the FRG.
1961-1989: Berlin was divided by wall.
1990: Germany is reunited.

Index